So I Began

So I Began

Lisa Lubasch

SOLID OBJECTS

NEW YORK

First edition, 2014

Printed in the United States of America

Grateful acknowledgment is made to the editors of the following publications,
in which this work first appeared, occasionally in a slightly different form:

"The Situation/Evidence" and "A sounding at the ear" in *A Public Space*; "come to
me, sweet stranger" in *The Awl*; "So I Began" in *Black Clock* (opening 3 sections)
and *Volt* (complete poem); "Getting Around It" in *Boston Review*; "This Now"
and "you have come, seeking" in *Colorado Review*; "She conceals what she," "in
the sun it is a face of a figure," "One day," "Starts like a summit or a vowel" in
Denver Quarterly.

ISBN-13: 978-0-9844142-5-3
ISBN-10: 0-9844142-5-8

Library of Congress Control Number: 2013942511

5 4 3 2

SOLID OBJECTS
P. O. Box 296
New York, NY 10113

So I Began

One

This Now

But would not rest,
But would not rest the day upon the hand,
Where the stars would signify,
Where the craft of leaving would unearth,
Where, bleed
This is one,
This one
In the effort, and the one of the effort,
And the one of the music,
And the one of the screen
These are the vertical drawings,
These, inside the crate of moving targets,
These rows and blanks and particles,
These names of the green vanquishments

So in lines of telling,
So in lines,
One line of the lines of strategies

Where the thought is dragged,
Where it betrays,
Where you can see the note of its returning,
The myth of it wasted

On the landing
And beyond, if nothing else
Can train the mind to listen,
Train it to hear

What, in words, would stifle,
What would lend
The no and yes to universal things

These suggested ends,
How ends would speak
Them and be heard.

The Situation/Evidence

Open hangs his head and begins to mumble.

I am not quite at that point, but in a moment I could be mumbling too.

I notice three things about this place.

The first is that Open inhabits it.

The second thing I notice is that I—I—

The third thing develops as the light moves down the tumbling place. . . .

The tumbling place is my name for—

One of the things that tumbles into the tumbling place is our—

Believe me or not, we have been held up here for hours.

At least three hours I would estimate, yes.

Three hours begins to seem like a lot more hours when you have no provisions or sealed medications.

Provisions and sealed medications were promised us, from the outset.

From the outset Open was skeptical. He said, Cheat (that is my name), he said, Cheat, we got no time to do this.

By this Open meant travel on the sly.

I might have agreed with Open, had my mother, Amelia, not decided it was time to remove my favorite white chemise from the little banister on which it had been hanging since my adolescence.

Into the garbage it went.

Or perhaps not the garbage but the garden.

I have still not recovered from the loss of Chemie to the garden.

Chemie, my chemise.

Three hours ago Open and I were in much better shape.

Open is mumbling with his head hanging down.

I decide not to bother him.

With my arms hanging low I struggle in my bondage suit through the white crackle of the evening.

Who knows where I am going, and why the evening is white.

I arrive at a tree and I rest.

I can see Open in the distance, his head hanging low, his bondage suit making it tough for him to follow me.

I wouldn't have wanted him to follow me, even if he could have. I am ripe for a bit of solitude, the white crackle of the pine cones, that sort of thing.

I suppose Amelia is looking for me by now, I suppose she has been wondering where I've disappeared to, and why.

I bet she regrets ever dumping my chemise.

From this angle I can see Open. I can see his long thick persecuted stare, heavy as a humpback's, trailing off through the distance.

I can see him pushing out against his bondage suit.

I also want to push out against my bondage suit.

I want to push out and I am in a slightly better position than Open to do this.

For one thing my head isn't hanging yet.

That's because my medications are still working, while Open's medications are not.

It's evident, one, from the hanging of his head, and two, from the way he is spastically pushing out against his bondage suit, accomplishing nothing.

I feel sorry for Open, but I know I'm going to be in a similar position if provisions and medications do not arrive soon.

From my position at the tree I say a short prayer.

O Lord, forgive me.

What I know is the levers on my spine have not reached nearly as serious an angle as the levers on Open's spine.

The levers, which are possibly responsible for his mumbling?

I give a little start. It is not a big start but a little start. Just enough of a start to be appropriate to the level of the pain that arrives in my right side, like the poking of a carapace.

What I need now is a little paregoric.

But do I get a little paregoric?

No, I do not get a little paregoric, obviously, because the medications that should have arrived three hours ago are still not here, not as they were promised us.

I shout across the distance to Open.

Nothing, no response, just as I expected.

I am assuming Open is a goner. The levers on his spine are forcing him into a dreadful low position.

Do I have regrets?

Maybe.

Do I have dreams past?

And yet, even with the tumbling place in my line of sight, even with Open struggling on the sectioned landing just before the tumbling place, I refuse to give in to the hopelessness of the situation.

I have this situation, and no other. . . .

Getting Around It

First thing you do is get around it. It is a hard thing to get around but the way you do it you are able to get around it.

It is a difficult thing to get around.

Next thing you do is reel it in. In and under. You reel it in.

That's also difficult so it is good that you succeed, reeling it in.

When you have managed to get around it and have succeeded in reeling it in, what you do next is consider it.

You consider it briefly.

But you cannot live with yourself considering it.

You cannot live with yourself considering it but you have to live with yourself. You have no one else to live with.

So you say to yourself, If I must live with myself then I will try to consider that I have made progress. I have made considerable progress. Not many people know.

Not many people know, but that doesn't detract from the progress. Who needs people to know? you say.

What you say next is, I do?

But you quickly dismiss that as the thought of a person who has not made progress.

Not as much progress as you have made.

Anyway, all this considering of your progress has made you a little nervous. And so you go back to reeling it in.

When that's done you try again to get around it.

Not this time.

No way of getting around it. This time.

. . . . . . And yet . . . .

. . . . Could there be some kind of way?

Absolutely not, no way.

Back to reeling it in.

In and under. You reel it in.

Eventually this leads to feelings of boredom. So much boredom that you give up reeling it in and go back to considering it briefly.

More than once you have tried this, could not live with it, and have had to boost yourself up by considering your progress.

You are sick of boosting yourself up by considering your progress.

It is awful to boost.

What is there to boost?

No more boosting.

You have squandered your progress with boosting.

Is there nothing else to do?

Other than getting around it, reeling it in, considering it briefly, and boosting yourself up by considering your progress, you cannot think of much.

Wait. . . . .

. . . . . . *hmmmmmm* . . . .

You could extrapolate?

Extrapolate?

Yes, you could extrapolate a pattern from the progress you have made. That's not quite boosting yourself up but is figuring something out instead.

OK, so you set yourself up to figure something out.

You gather yourself into a posture and begin to figure something out.

You extrapolate. . . . .

But nothing much is figured out.

Only that you have six toes on one foot and just three on the other.

How did this happen?

Oh my God.

Figuring something out is even worse than boosting yourself up, as it turns out.

Having abandoned this last activity you really don't have anything significant left.

You are done extrapolating, that's for sure. For a brief moment you consider boosting yourself up by considering your progress but then you remember where that led you.

Suddenly out of nowhere you see a beautiful metal gurney rolling in the distance.

You consider it briefly.

Then you reel it in.

In and under.

You strap yourself with some plastic things onto the metal gurney.

There is no way of getting around it, you think.

The gurney keeps rolling with you on it. You with the plastic straps on the metal gurney. You say a bedtime prayer you have memorized from childhood and then lapse into sleep.

In the morning, the gurney has been parked, and someone comes to wake you up.

It is no one you recognize.

First thing you do is count your toes. . . . .

Six and three, just as you remember.

. . . . Just as you remember . . . only a little bit different.

One of your toes has some letters written on it.

Once the someone who has come to wake you up has left the room, you name the letters aloud.

The letters do not add up to much.

I do not want these letters, you think, cutting off that toe.

You cut off the toe and dispose of it in a little wagon that has appeared next to the gurney.

Then you make a tourniquet, that is not a problem.

The tourniquet is made of materials.

Each morning you proceed like this, amputating one toe that has been newly written on with letters and disposing of it in the wagon.

Then you make a tourniquet with materials.

Someone who comes to wake you up appears not-bothered by the accumulation of toes.

You are not so bothered either.

What you are is ready to get around it.

Ready or not, you have no toes left.

Just like that you stand up. It's hard to stand without your toes. You are really not used to standing without them.

Can you live with yourself considering that you have lost all your toes?

You're still deciding.

Considering it and deciding.

Since you long ago abandoned boosting yourself up with obsolete notions of progress, you figure it could go either way.

It Was

in absence, by light
of moon, with nothing
but an orifice

she refused to dance,
dancing only for escape,
as love is but a question,

but a question, but a ringing
in her ear,
fear to wager, what is lost

Feb. –

A sounding at the ear.   And a ringing at the doorstep.   Look,
she said, a sounding at my hair, and a laughing in the footsteps.
A terrible laughing.   Certainly is terrible, and certainly is
honorable.   Better to be honorable than eligible.   Or
perhaps not eligible at all.   *The name fell twice.   It was (the*
substance of the name she heard).   (The substance or the distance
from it.)   Redundant knocking.   A drift, a birch, through
daylight, lost.   Drifting, drifting, into stalwart dawn.   We
are measuring its aperture.   Deep rose, written into English.
Written into daylight.   One by one.

come to me, sweet stranger, and make of me a moment, a nostalgia, to give to the wind, to give to the one, who is standing there, at the meeting place, where the safety is immense, and not to tangle with, where the sentence can arrive, as though through a spaciousness, surrounding her, through its particulars, through its split, integument, intangible, what she will take, what she will have, to wander, with, over the paths, with their names in tow, in time, a morning, a motive,

come to me, sweet stranger, and make of me a ruthlessness, out of the fatigue, a furlough or a breathlessness, to gather into the hands, to hone or hammer, hurry, though, redemptive, as the gaze, untraceable, as the contagion,

come to me, sweet stranger, and make of me a henceforth, further, I am willing to make it one, pronounceable, convinced of its own, utter, patternlessness, through the wave, of inhumanity, throughout, the future,

come to me, sweet stranger, and make of me a yearning, out of the likelihood, a line, to splinter, upwards, nearly, through the enlightenment, through its trance, of tears, through barrenness, whiteness, to seize, the abruptness,

come to me, sweet stranger, and make of me a timing, to tow a way with, to rival, like catastrophe, as if starting back from, to take away, foolishness, from the beginning, from loneliness, from the atrocity,

come to me, sweet stranger, and make of me a lightness, a music,
sweeps through, much in the way of, wonder, originates, on the
whim, which collapses, underneath the weight, where there was
none, to arrange, to redeem,

throughout, to begin with, tenderness

letter to say that she can come

    now one, now the other

          wanders

               under a canopy
               under a whiteness

So I began to dismantle it.   It was near a temple.   A figure
drawn off.   Towards the end.   Through.   Miraculous.
Yes – tolling.   Term she gave.   What spoken.   So I began.
It took days.   To reach the.   Say.   It does not matter.   So
boundless is the trying.   She came from the temple.   Arrived
from there.   A wanderer, perhaps.   No, not in this weather.
Words she spoke.   Had the quality of.   A question.   To
answer no other.   In what she was.   Having to pronounce.

Not a telling, but a faltering.   Through trees her sight fell, upon.
A figure drawn off towards.   Light.   It does not matter.
Looking in the matter.   Luminous the hill.

Through trees, her lips.   Instilled a question.   Not sending,
landing.   Placed me here, and I fell to it, upon it.   It was as if
reversed.   Figure drawn off.   The quality of, it was.

Measured.   Implored, opened upon.   Like the sun, or a
diagonal.   Ceasing.   And unversing itself.   Melting.
Fluidity.

A dent.   Making a shallow, zero.   Gone inside.   One apart.
Thought: Its separated call.   Which trace.   Almost inscribed.
A permanence of sorts.   To name.   Infirm.

You fancy yourself like.   But you are not.   Like what?
Ungestured in the slaughter.   Over the line.   Itself alone.
Last and first.   Unscoring a location.   So I took off in a
direction.   No form to.   Decampment.

Trenchant.   Marching.   Released from.   After birth.   The
disciple resting.   Enfolded.   Flood beneath.   Deracinated
sentry.   Never to emblazon.   A cord.   The being late.
Disannulled.   To tell of her.   Devotions.   To.   Flourish in.

Where to go.

it doesn't harbor, resilience,

it won't mend, inside, rebuild,

of the water, the will

to resist, like sentiment,

she wants it to find her, say her name before, she wants it to, tear

what comes, inhibitory,

she wants it to slash,
to convince

Two

Pour drops in the mouth. Wait for. Coat the tongue. Wait for the regulated breath. Return. Wait for the. Silence. To come. You hold your breath. Waiting for the. Silence.

untied   from the
allegory

Starts like a summit or a vowel. There inside it. She cannot go anywhere. Out. Is out of the question. Elsewhere. Out of the question. She cannot swear. Besides. It doesn't help anymore. She cannot speak. Their answers. What they want. Is obvious. Is it not. It's raining. It is summer. It is warm, like hands. Possible sketch of the future, of maturity?

And when it happens there is no explanation. It keeps going on like days in the. Foolishly waits. For someone's words. Foolishly waits. For a time or a task. Another to begin. The first one. Is that what you are waiting for?

Resuscitated as a kind of unrest. Blade. Slowly. Blown slowly. Over it. It is not anyone. It isn't you. Someone in the hardened room suspends a deaf recitation. You are alone, but someone inquires. Have you been through the [exit]?

The age she is. Entered. Information. Is acquired. Specifications. Height. Weight. The hour of. Injury. It proceeds according to an ornate. Assumption. The words she chooses. Are too vulnerable. Respond. Only. According to. Need.

A flashlight shines. In the middle of the night. Into the eyes. (The light becomes a kind of riot. Unclassifiable. Instant.)

No one can indicate the terms. Point to them. Entering. Into you.

A brutalizing structure. Attempts to. You are 'taken advantage of'
because you are 'perceived' as victim, unable to mark a pattern
within your own emotionless. Ardor. Unable to. Concentrate. Within
a vector. Around a vein.

'Suspect' from the start. An evaporated. Color. Like the color of
precipitation. Or an intensity. 'Reasoning.'

The structure replicates around her. Its efforts. To compartmentalize, assign a cadence to its armor. Its mode of operating – 'power' – 'not letting' ('in the logic of')

*

the air, the particle
too minute, to harbor

everything that comes,
holds its being, its name

to spit out, how I became thou,
or you became thus,

stays in her throat,
stalking her, contrite,

tearful, absorbing it,
mouthfuls, she strays through

the window, throughout the memory,
arrives, has names for all, she

imagines, the speech,
the arms

are held back, without a
shiver, infatuation

to incur (incursive),
the trigger, insensible, softer,

the trees, together,
never grow upwards

her words are others' words, she is sure of it, she is alone but together,
with the others here, though not at home, no time for anything but
care of the body, which she attempts to keep together, whole, like the
sun, before it was gone, no time to think, to rest,

the inclination, of others,
is to treat as oddity,

seed the neglect, with inquiries,
as if to enlarge, repeat,

anything, its way,
the whimper, to control,

as though blindly

Without the thought of love, the whole idea is useless. It begins. She imagines it. Beginning. The thought of. Love. The thought. As form. Of otherness. Of beginning. She went this way. And outside herself. From the stance of all that happens.

Opening. Out. Into the air. It is a fullness. Through. She is given some kind of stencil. Not to retrieve the. Letter. It won't exist. Outside of 'friendship,' outside of 'form.' Where here there is none? 'In' here. (Or where there will be, but only later, as a portion of the memory.)

It points. Into a separateness. The separation is from her name. In what they try to structure. Is an out. Language is the 'mark.' One cannot draw the path. From here to the notation. No remark. But time to take it. As if to remember.

*she develops methods, for tracing sensation, movement, for
monitoring, function, the transcription of moments, rapidly,
becoming, what's left, through her, another, measure*

`when the sun enters

      `it is to / scatter freely

in the sun it is a face of a figure, it is transported. towards. no one
in the room can see herself in the observer. is that a symptom or
an aspect of some blind, unnamed 'ambivalence'? it's not up to you
to 'name' or to conceal, now you are the protest of an incandescing
[term]

One day. One day soon, you say. And for now you are in the next room and can only hear. This much of. What is a memory? What is a memoir? My own room so far away in the backdrop like a piece of some displaced vernacular. Want to say. What for. Wait for.

Wait for. What. Not an aleph or bet. You stand as a night form. You encourage a kind of stammering. Out of. Off of the air a sigh not wished for. Is like a caved in word. Like a transgression. You want to go towards it.

*

like a sharpness, to marry, the stillness, the lullaby, with silence, with
the rite, with kindness

you have come, seeking refuge, resuscitated, not once, but twice, the air is yours, the earth is, filled with compassion, it does not know, its rescue, relief, moral, inclination, you have gone, past, confused, your occupation, with that of a contestant, whose activities, you memorize, like patterns, to consume,

you are a plot, you are a trance, a blankness, you have collaborated on the calamity, ignorant of consequence, difference worries you, yet you are willing to go along, try your hand at anything, as long as it is, within the parameters,

you are an outsider, and your fate has been determined by the gate-keepers, there is no rest, not for you or for others, and your time here is up, reached its mark, its mistake, has come to its resting place, with your back turned to it, as though to all,

your oppression is, and your mouth is a handful of wool, and your features others' features, you have prepared your children, by making them, routine, to stare at the screen with infatuation,

a heroine, your country, gone the way, of, even without the names, of those, consumed, by the system, amassed, hardly a day passes, hardly a time, a fragment, or considered, response is given, mention,

you've held, in the hallways, their hands, you've kissed, the detachments,
without consideration, of one who has been, carried here, alone, with
truth, without exaggeration, evidence, without the remorse,

the assistance, of the one who gave birth, a refusal, of everything,
that has ever come upon,

like retrieval, like solace, like rest

`[as if one is] [confined to gesture only] (embrace?)

*

in the text she dresses in two coats, one navigates towards the other, its shyness evident in, lashes, [labors]

the subject [rejoins the host]

you need the book but it isn't anywhere – elsewhere an other a
fervor itself like an ailment or intrusion – when you say something
to someone, it is against this ailment, like strands of the person not
coming forth but meaning to

and without it you feel barren [reciprocality impossible?] like
speaking an answer to   her [when she was there]   and you
are embolic like summer

so you sketch a kind of whim, go to the left, a little more, and no one
is distracted, now quickly you are away from it, from them, from

*loss of the present. is there a moment when you don't think how
it was then? erosion of the present, or a constant remainder in the
[sensation][of the present]   and almost everything of* substance
*dissipates, so that all you can (almost) hear is the concerned
brightness of a star, a measured out aporia,*

*even yesterday the sense of no one watching, no one thinking, no
one behaving, no one as afraid as* you have been,

impossible [impossible?] to feel that kind of fear again. or is that
what you feel now, *a kind of homage to an error*

does not see, what becomes,
what is, try, to answer,
the incarceration, wearing,

but oneself, as if she were,
without, she wants to ask,
of the injustice, doesn't have,

capacity, is too slow, to terms,
to others, she resembles, what
others are, that

she resembles no one, nothing
she recalls ever having been,
as if taken out, unable to give,

to release

Is she weakened, or contrite? What is her name? How do these
surroundings. Examine her? Observe her? What do her 'questions'
'say.' Of them?

      Or are they looking only for fear?

        a thread, rather

the air

     whose trespass

       the perch
          exposed

of silence, lack of any human vow?

trying to decide whether or not to send the letter and this idea keeps coming up at the margins, that there could be no one to receive it, no voice

you wait for the weather to pass, you immerse yourself in the transient, better to be filled with it

people – I say 'people' knowingly – like to describe the outside [could outside be / a summons / or is it just a word?]

*

over the line, and past,

over the sentence,

keeps you, until you, go,

with the others, unwillingness

inch, not past

it won't repair, over, contentiousness,

go, with the others, unwillingness,

don't move an inch, not past,

over the line, to step

you haven't, taken the vow, to encounter,

is not, illustrious, here,

allow, the conjecture

light, same, tremor

over the sentence

keeps you,

the vow

its opening

past, willingness,

not without a try

this narrowing, after,

after, this

this life

`for some people – it is like – turning / off / the / switch /
`relief ? /

in front of them – positionless address

`having trouble locating / self /

`like tears /

`still very fragile /

`what is hurting self / and how different is the / hurting self /
from it?

`just sit quietly / and wait

`swallow

`emboldened by the / door

`god help us

`and summer is / the spot on /

`the easier / to place

`it comes off as naïve /
    exemplum

  `but the switch /
is /

  `anyway /

`what is 'good' for me /

`don't have time to say to

`everything time / and
slack-ish /

`and this / no / better

`if you could get inside of it

`foolish

`metaphor

`but even that's not true

to transfer,

the, happening,

this a, lessening,

a reverence,

at every, touch

(each)

*

If they imprison. If they charge. If torture, the torture is incessant.
Name it. To still. To protect.

Press the retrieval. Of memory. Press numbers. Dial. Call up. Call up one. Say. Say, still. Then, wait.

`ask for Human /

`no Human /

`ask for substitute /

`no substitute /

ask for

She conceals what she imagines are the implications of her personal history. Time contained. Within a quarry of seconds. She cannot count them. Each is like an entrance, towards which there is no possible imbricated arc. The sanctity of her version. Which one discards in disbelief. They tend to speak at once.

`*questioning / of the / 'stabilizing' figure  [authoritarian]*`

                    `*[out of context], consigned to the*`
       `*laboratory /*`

                  "outcomeless"

Noting it like

'Any day now the tides will turn'

`and you can / disrupt . suffering / but not / without /

        – a terrible – or enterprising – joke

dull cry in the figural distance – who is that? is that you? and you protect it / but it's constantly taken away / no metaphor for that / not even a sense that ['time will tell']

at night no one sleeps; one searches through the variants,
in [which] [utterance]

[there may be a border around it]

.

These. 'Rights.' Dissolve. No one can. Restore you. No one hear the quick. Renunciation.

A. Poignant. Philosophy. That the lectern. The nearest. Person. Would 'act.' To irrigate. The wound. Would couple. With a. Genuine. Openness. Who is. Wounded. And. Not wounded. At the same time?

Inside. Spindle. Like.

Can be joined. (Or. Cannot be.)

This within the /

walls

      where one would [try]

Seep in.   Obeisance,

        'fragility.'

They put them in chemical restraints.

Rejoice.

       Dispensary.

Place. Subject.

             Chase its. Volume.

less [noticeable]

                    enters;

           `*unable to*   *guess*

`recedes [as if to precede a statement]

`[notices / uneven edges]

`lapse like pain in the head /
she has trouble / differentiating

moves over and against,   moves through but does not

nourish,

not to succumb

your faith is letter

dissolves into a medicine

[of   investigation]

wakes to a sparseness

that the whole thing could be un-said like some sort of denouncement
could be

abounds

LISA LUBASCH is the author of four previous collections of poetry, including *Twenty-One After Days* (Avec Books), a selection from which received a PIP Gertrude Stein Award for Innovative Poetry in English. Her other books are *To Tell the Lamp*, *Vicinities*, and *How Many More of Them Are You?*, which received the Norma Farber First Book Award from the Poetry Society of America. She is also the translator of Paul Éluard's *A Moral Lesson* (Green Integer). Her work has been translated into French and appears as part of Un bureau sur l'Atlantique's *Format Américain* series.